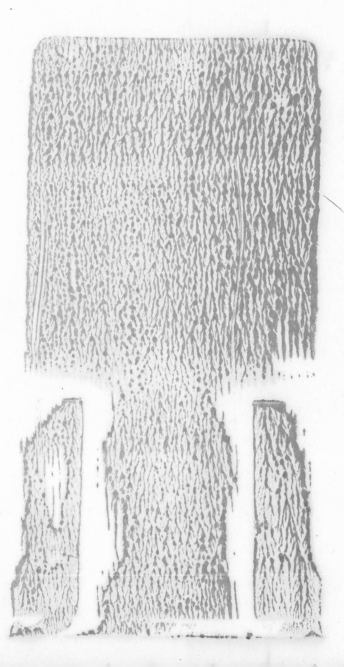

DIRECT WAX SCULPTURE

DIRECT WAX

CHILTON BOOK COMPANY

SCULPTURE

by *Frank Eliscu*

PHOTOGRAPHS BY DAVID ROSENFELD

PHILADELPHIA · NEW YORK · LONDON

Published in Philadelphia by Chilton Book Company
and simultaneously in Ontario, Canada,
by Thomas Nelson & Sons, Ltd.
Library of Congress Catalog Card Number 71-102050
Designed by Harry Eaby
Manufactured in the United States of America by
Vail-Ballou Press, Inc.

To the memory of a wonderful friend, Harrison Tweed,
who would have enjoyed seeing this book
and the fruition of the work he helped nourish.

ACKNOWLEDGMENTS

My gratitude and appreciation to the many friends and associates whose help made possible the writing of this book. Among the many are Dorothy Mallen, for a perfect typing job from a perfectly illegible manuscript. Alfred Easton Poor, for the use of the wax eagle I made for him, and so called it "Poor's Eagle." Dan Hudak and the entire staff of The General Casting Company, for the use of their facilities in The Centrifugal Casting chapter. And, of course, all of the sculptors and their galleries who so kindly permitted the use of their work in this book.

CONTENTS

DIRECT WAX SCULPTURE

FOREWORD

It is only recently that wax as a medium for sculpture has assumed its cloak of respectability and is now being rediscovered by sculptors. Although it is one of the oldest and most sensitive of sculptural media, its very versatility and adaptability have led it into some strange byways in the three dimensional field.

From the waxes of Benvenuto Cellini to the wax moulage figures of Madame Toussaud's Museum, there runs a gamut of all styles and tastes.

Who can look at a Degas ballerina in a wax and then a bowl of wax fruit without marveling at the incongruity of both being conceived through the same medium? In the hands of an artist, wax captures every nuance of the sculptor's intention, and its sense of immediacy gives it a freshness and sparkle that accounts for its new popularity as a sculptural medium.

To those of you who are looking for an "open sesame" to the appreciation of sculpture by doing sculpture, this book should help. To those who seek happiness by doing something creative, you've found the right volume. And to those who wish to add a new technique to an already familiar repertoire, good luck!

Now, as to you others who are looking for an "instant sculpture" kit, I'm sorry, but there is just no such thing. However, don't close this book yet because there is this one little thing I forgot to tell you. The hardest part of all art is starting. We are usually so intimidated by the mystique of "art" that we are insecure about the whole thing before we even start.

If you feel brave enough to get your feet wet, take one little step and try one of the simple projects. If it looks like anything, you are off to a start. There are no "artsy craftsy" projects in this book. The work is on a professional level, but the definition of a professional in the art world leaves lots of room. A dedication to work, an imagination, plus the knowledge of how to can take you to the start! Remember, if what you have done in this medium is a tangible expression of your concept, that is all that matters. And your work is responsible to no one but yourself.

A famous artist, when told that his painting did not look like a woman, answered, "Madam, this is not a woman, this is a painting." Get the point? So get started!

THE MEDIUM

It is believed that the first form of art in the world was sculpture. Even before cave painting, man formed things with his hands. First he found that soft clay from the river beds was easily shaped into container-like forms, or pots, and then he went on to experimenting with stone and wood, and Man, the Sculptor, formed weapons. As the utilization of these objects increased, his inventiveness demanded individuality in shapes and design.

Once the basic needs of survival were taken care of, man turned to making just things. Using whatever nature supplied in the way of material, he shaped the things that were of concern to him. Gods to be worshiped made of wood or of stone, clay figurines recording a hunt, he used whatever was available to fulfill his urge to leave his own message—not in spoken words, lost on the wind, but in a medium of permanence and capable of telling more graphically than words a personal observation or belief.

As the centuries flew by, man's only record of his life and times were those artifacts and primitive wall decorations that survived time. But man had by this time learned to use many new materials supplied by nature, and to leave a more sophisticated imprint of his culture. Clay was baked into terra-cotta, stones were polished by water, sand was formed into glass, and wax was not only found malleable, but was also a vehicle used as a transition step to making gold or metal castings.

An interesting sidelight into the use of wax is the origin of the word "sincere." The dictionary gives the meaning of the word as "pure, unmixed, honest." The Latin meaning of the word is *sin* (without) and *cire* (wax), "without wax." It seems that the Romans, when casting in bronze or other metals, often disguised small flaws in the castings by filling them with wax. And so into usage came the word "sincere."

The most famous of the workers in wax as we know it has to be Benvenuto Cellini, who wrote his story of the casting of the Medusa in *cire-perdue*, or lost wax method, which incidentally is used today with virtually no changes in the process. The original Perseus by Cellini done in direct wax is now on exhibit at the Bargello Museum in Florence,

Italy, and the wax has retained all the spontaneity and freshness of the sculptor's hands.

Like everything else, wax as a medium for sculpture has had its periods of popularity, then giving way to other media. But over the years nothing has ever been found to replace it as the material for capturing nuances of modeling demanding delicacy combined with comparative tensile strength.

The microcrystallines used today are, of course, petroleum products and, as such, synthetic waxes. But to all intents and purposes they work exactly the same as beeswax. In fact, with modern technology they are better than the original beeswax, as they can be made as hard or soft as desired. Some waxes (microcrystalline) used in industrial or jewelry work seem as hard as glass when not melted. Think of the advantage of controlling the wax; some sculptors like a "summer wax" or a "winter wax." And so today, wax is not only an "accepted" medium but is extensively used because it gives a wide leeway for individual inventiveness and personalized technique.

WHAT WAX IS

WAX: A yellow solid of animal origin, excreted by bees from the abdominal rings. Beeswax.

It has a honey-like odor and a balsamic taste. It becomes plastic with the heat of the hand; has a specific gravity of 0.951 to 0.960 at 25° C., and a melting point of 62° to 64° C.; is insoluble in water, but almost completely dissolved by boiling alcohol.

So reads the dictionary definition of wax. It is important to know exactly what we are working with, its properties, its potentials and its limitations. For us, the phrase, "becomes plastic with the heat of the hand" is the open door to a new sculptural medium.

I first started working with wax when I was very young, ten years old in fact. My great-grandmother, who lived with us, was in the habit of burning a type of religious candle made of paraffin in a thick glass. There was always an inch or so of paraffin left in the bottom of the glass, and so with the curiosity of the young I experimented by taking this residue paraffin into the bathtub and softening it in the warm water. In fact, I modeled my first masterpiece this way—a horse's head (a white, Arabian Stallion, of course, for wasn't Rudolph Valentino the rage as the Sheik!).

My father, taking an interest in the results of my unusual pastime, searched for a "wax" that was not as slippery as paraffin, for that was my basic complaint.

He found that drugstores used pure beeswax—I think it was used as a base for making certain unguents—and it is still available in some drug stores today. Thus I found a wax that seemed to work by itself.

I was thrilled at ten years of age, and now, many, many years later, I get the same thrill in feeling the response of the wax to my fingers. I used beeswax for many years and felt that it was unbeatable—and it is. It is second only to microcrystalline—a synthetic wax—actually an outgrowth of paraffin.

Historically speaking, the petroleum wax, known as paraffin, has been used for about fifty years. Microcrystalline is a contemporary product which was developed in the 1920's.

Both paraffin and microcrystalline originate by boiling crude oil and are produced by a highly sophisticated distillation technique. This process produces lubricating oils and waxes by a very complicated operation, much of the oil being removed from the wax by crystallization. Finally, the de-oiled wax is purified to remove color and odor bodies and to produce a tasteless, odorless, and colorless product. This, in essence, (and as nontechnical as I can make it) is microcrystalline.

So microcrystalline is wax, and a substitute for beeswax. It will do all that beeswax does, and for the purpose of this book, beeswax and microcrystalline are the same.

BUYING WAX

While everyone knows what wax is, very few people know where to procure wax that is suitable for modeling.

Because sculptors have begun using this medium more frequently, and the demand has made it commercially feasible, Mobil Oil Company now has a "wax for sculpture" called "Modeling Wax, Formula 2300." This is sold in fifty or hundred pound quantities and is quite inexpensive. This so-called wax is really a microcrystalline—a petroleum product with exactly the same qualities of beeswax, but far better for sculpture as it is constant in quality. (Beeswax varies according to the flowers the bees gathered it from, etc.) Also, it can be purchased in various hardnesses, i.e., a summer wax or a winter wax.

Formula 2300 can be purchased from Mobil Oil Company or one of its franchising dealers. Most large art stores now carry modeling wax, or a letter to Mobil Oil Company will direct you to a franchised dealer.

In the Yellow Pages of the New York City telephone directory, under Waxes, there are dozens of concerns that advertise Beeswaxes, Modeling Waxes, Sculpturing Waxes, etc., so the problem of where to get wax should give you no trouble.

THE WAYS OF WORKING WAX

Every artist has his preferred way of working wax. The basic property of wax is its reaction to climate. It will, in a warm temperature, become malleable and plastic, then when plunged into cold water will harden immediately. And when in contact with flame or heat it will melt.

Some artists work with an alcohol lamp or candle flame; some warm the wax in a bowl of hot water; some use the warmth of the sun, or even the slight heat from a radio, if the pieces of wax are on the radio over where the tubes warm the cabinet top. And some, like myself, use all these methods as they are needed.

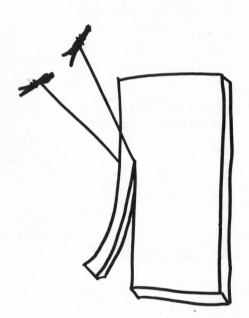

All workers in wax will need a source of flame, an alcohol lamp or candle and a spatula or knife that can be heated in the flame. An alcohol lamp is preferable to a candle, as the carbon from the candle flame will smoke and blacken the wax.

A marble top table is nice to work on, but not very much better than any good kitchen tabletop.

To cut pieces from a very large slab of wax, you can use a wire with handles—clothes pins, or anything comfortable to hold. (Wax is very difficult to cut in large pieces.)

Rolling pin and sponge for rolling out large sheets—the sponge is to dampen the roller and the surface rolled upon so that the wax will not stick to the surface or roller.

TOOLS

The tools for direct wax sculpture are simple, basic, and easily obtainable.

Let's list the actual necessities, and then go on from there. First, of course, a knife to cut wax—a scout knife is fine, or a kitchen knife is also excellent. But always a knife that comes to a point, because a butter knife or one with a rounded end cannot get into small delicate areas.

Not a tool, but a necessity for wax sculpture, we must include a source of heat. The best, of course, is an alcohol lamp, but if it's not available, an ordinary candle will do. Incidentally, plumber's candles—those thick tallow candles—last the longest.

The actual tools for modeling the wax are optional. They can be as simple as sharpened pencils (which should not be scoffed at; they're pretty good) to the elaborate rosewood and ebony modeling tools that many sculptors use.

In between these two extremes are the ordinary Turkish boxwood modeling tools, available in any art store.

Steel tools, which are called "Fine Wax and Retouching" tools are available in the sculptural supply houses. These tools are excellent for use with your alcohol lamp or candle flame.

Very often it is possible to get some old dental tools. These steel tools are probably the most desirable, if you can get some. Ask your dentist if he has some old, blunted, or even broken tools, for these are perfectly good for wax.

Not a tool by any means but a definite aid to wax work is a block of wood with a wire, heavy enough to hold a wax, inserted into the wood. This will hold your statue and leave both your hands free for working.

Rolling pins, double boilers, copper wire, and the dozen other pieces of equipment needed are not really tools. For tools are, or should be, extensions of your fingers. So I will not include these various items.

THE FIRST STEPS

The first step in any technique is always the most difficult, and as in walking, the first steps are easier if one is helped. Then practice plus experience do the rest.

The Mouse

Small pieces of wax are cut from the large block in order to get workable pieces.

We soften our small pieces of wax in a bowl of warm water.

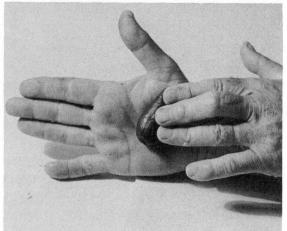

The softened wax is rolled in the hands.

A child can approach an art form more easily than an adult, for he is not intimidated by the word "ART," and is more apt to express his thoughts in any new medium in the simplest forms.

Before we can run, we must walk, so let us do something simple to give us the feel of the wax and free us from the inhibitions of using a new medium.

TOOLS

The less complicated the tools, the easier the work, and so with an ordinary kitchen or penknife, for cutting, an orange stick (as used for care of the nails) or a pencil sharpened in a pencil sharpener (for an even point), and your ten fingers, we are ready to start.

[8]

Continue rolling until our wax is shaped like a pear.

A small triangle of wax, slightly cupped, is added to the pear.

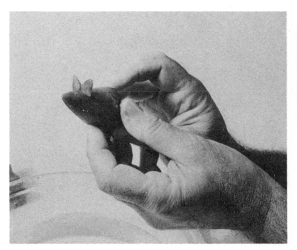

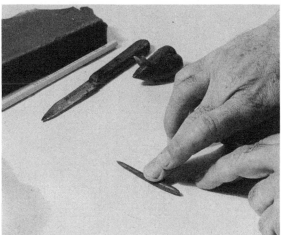

The other ear is added.

With a small piece of wax we roll out a tail.

1. Slice some pieces of wax from your large slab into small pieces in order to soften them more easily.

2. Then put these pieces of wax in a bowl or pan of warm water. The wax will soften in a very short time.

3. Take a piece of softened wax and roll it in your hands until it is shaped like a pear.

4. Take two little pieces of wax, form a couple of triangles. We will now put these on the pear and the pear becomes a mouse!

5. We take another piece of wax and roll it on a table in order to get a long tail for our mouse, and, of course, we add this onto the back of the mouse.

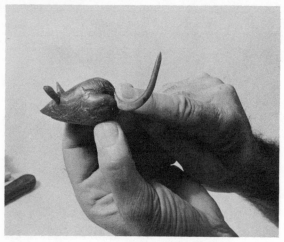

And, of course, we add it on to the back of our mouse, for by now it has assumed its identity.

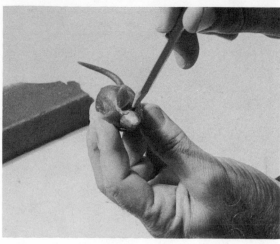

Using our pencil point, we make eyes by pressing the point into the soft wax.

Our mouse now sits contemplatively on a piece of wax, his tail curled around him.

By adding two front legs, we sit our mouse up, on a piece of stone.

6. With our sharpened pencil we make the eyes—*et voila*, a mouse!

With this one simple project, we have learned the basics of direct wax; i.e., softening the wax (one method), shaping the wax, attaching new pieces, adding detail.

And these are the first, but most important, steps.

School of Fish

We form some small cigar shaped pieces from the wax, which has been softened in a bowl of warm water.

We then flatten the small cigar shapes into flatter, fishlike forms.

A small crescent-shaped piece of wax, added on, becomes a tail.

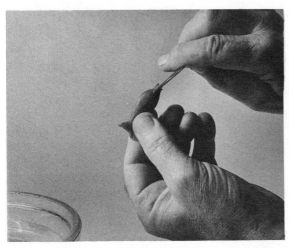

The other end, cut with a sharp knife, becomes the mouth.

With a ball for an eye, a fin under the gill, and a line across the length of the fish, we are ready to complete all four of our fish.

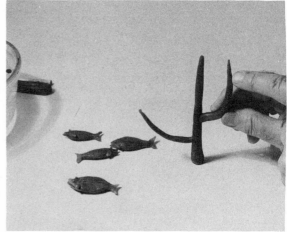

The fish now complete, we roll out some long, thin pieces for seaweed or coral forms.

The long pieces are put together to simulate sea growth.

The fish are attached to the seaweed in as interesting a pattern as can be made.

Using a candle and a hot tool, weld the seaweed and the fish together.

Here is the finished composition on a base. This type of sculpture, as easy as it is in wax, is most difficult in any other medium.

SHEET WAX TECHNIQUE

For working in larger forms, solid wax is an impractical medium, as well as being expensive, both as to the use of wax (a very small item) and the eventual casting in bronze (a large item).

Sheet wax is exactly what its name implies: thin, wafer-like sheets of wax, worked in the same way as sheet metal in welding is worked, but using wax on a frame instead of metal.

The thickness of the wax sheets will, of course, vary with the size of the project, and wax can be made (or even purchased) almost paper thin. Many dental supply firms sell wax sheets for dentists who use wax for models as a preliminary to gold or silver dental castings, usually centrifugally cast. These sheets are usually about 3″ x 5″ and are excellent for small models and experimental work.

The best method is, I believe, for an artist to run (or roll) his own sheets, according to what thickness is needed. Here are two techniques:
1. Prepare a surface on which to run your hot liquid wax. This can be a marble tabletop, a metal tabletop, or a similar surface, using any grease or oil, even salad oil. Make sure all the surface is moistened so the hot wax will not stick to it. Fence in the area where you wish the wax to stay, otherwise the wax will of course run over the table onto the floor. By fencing we mean enclosing with ruler, plasticine, slats of wood, or anything you can use to hold the wax in the area you want.
2. Melt your wax until it is liquid in a double boiler. Do not overcook wax, for when it is too hot it will start a boil and form bubbles. This is the reason for a double boiler. If melting wax in a pot or any can on a stove, watch it until all the lumps of wax have melted, then remove from the stove (or whatever form of heat you are using) before the heat has a chance to bubble the wax.
3. Slowly pour the wax into the fenced-in area until it is your desired thickness. I personally like a $1/16''$ to $1/8''$ thickness. The wax will cool in a few minutes and, of course, is readily separated from the oiled surface, ready for working.

Another method of making sheets of wax is the "rolling-out" technique.

First soften a large piece of wax in warm or fairly hot water. Then take two rulers, or any two pieces of wood, of the thickness you desire for your sheets of wax. Wet or oil your tabletop—water will do—wet your rolling pin so the wax won't stick to it and roll out the wax between the two wooden tracks.

Well, these are two methods, and any artist with imagination will come up with others. So do not be limited by these two simple techniques.

Supporting sheet wax sculpture calls for a sense of structure and ingenuity. Rods of wax may be used to reinforce the thin sheet where necessary. This reinforcement does more than just strengthen the wax; it will provide the necessary gates for the bronze flow in an eventual casting.

In these two prophets a sheet of wax was the basis for the figure. The heads, hands, etc., were added to give dimension to a flat shape.

Bird

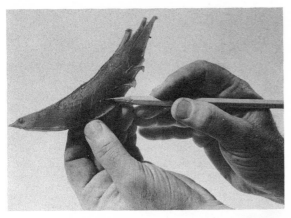

An ellipse is cut from a sheet of wax as in the preceding diagram—and bent over a rolling pin, or knife handle.

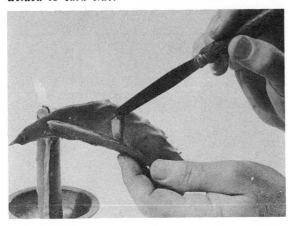

Eyes and feathers are modeled into the sheet, using any sharp tool. Below: A wax brace keeps the shape of the bird intact. With a hot tool the brace is welded to each side.

Legs are added and attached to the inside brace, and with heat welded together. Our bird now can stand.

A bronze of a bird, in which the thin sheets of wax are modeled into leaflike forms.

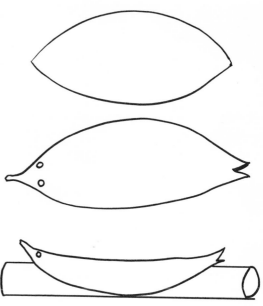

Butterfly

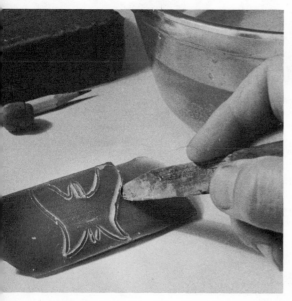

A sharp tool or knife cuts out the butterfly.

A butterfly is drawn on a thin piece of wax.

By pinching the soft wax the wings of the butterfly assume delicacy and shape.

The wings are curved up, around the pencil, and the butterfly is now three dimensional.

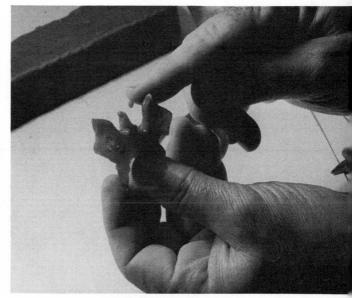

With our pencil point we pierce the wax to make a design that will give character to the butterfly.

Small beads of wax are added for eyes.

Antennae are added, and we now have cut, pierced, rolled and attached wax, to make a butterfly.

The wax butterfly and a bronze done exactly the same way.

Head

Using a sheet of wax and a rubber ball. . . .

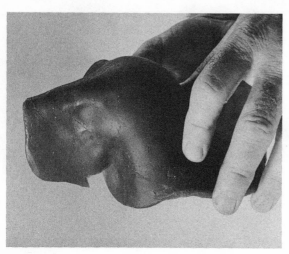

The pliable wax is shaped around the ball.

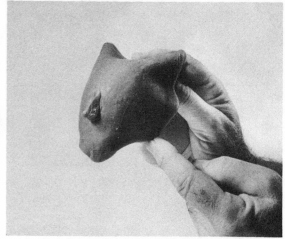

A triangle of wax on our oval mask of wax becomes a nose.

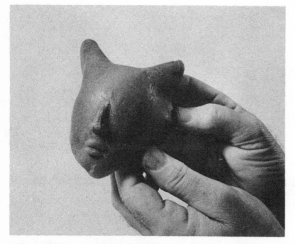

The addition of two small ellipse shaped pieces of wax form the lips.

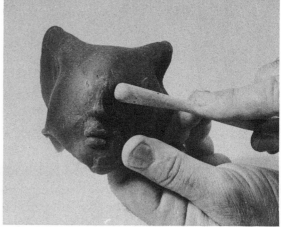

Using a rounded tool or your finger, indent the wax for an eye socket and brow.

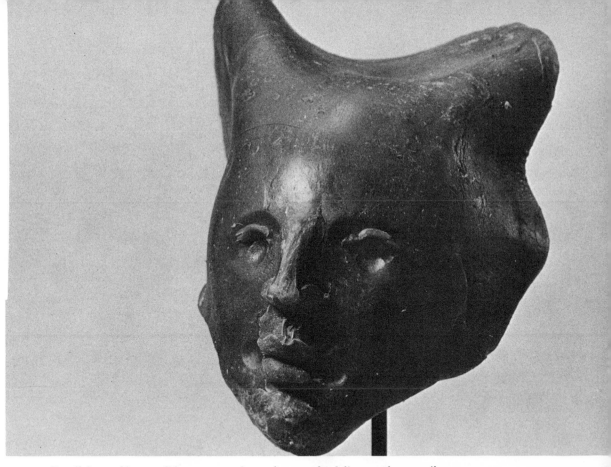

Detail by making eyelids, or eyes, shape the mouth, delineate the nostrils, etc.

The head in sheet wax seen in profile. The hair, ears, etc., can be made now if one wishes to carry this head on to completion.

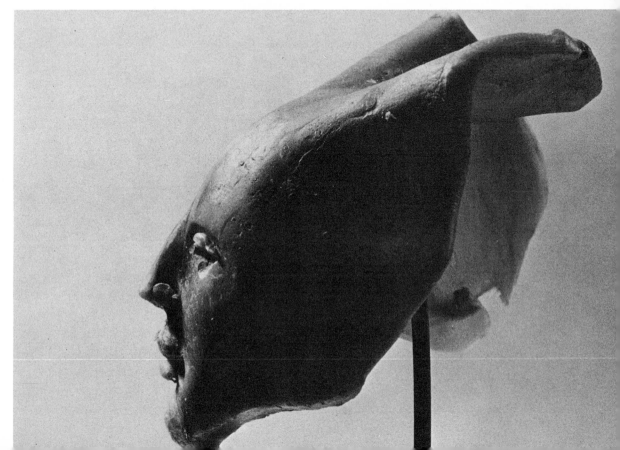

Lion

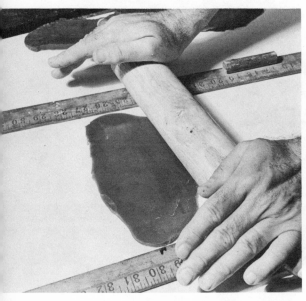

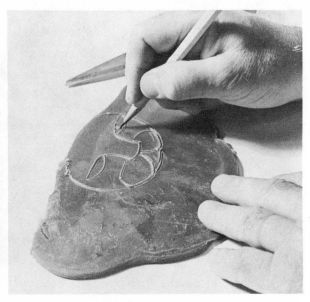

The softened wax is rolled into a thin sheet between two rulers—giving us an even ¼″ thickness—the same thickness as the rulers.

The head of a lion is drawn—or incised—on the flat sheet of wax.

The head is cut out of the sheet.

The detailing of the head—eyeballs and whiskers done with the sharp pencil point—and the mane added with small pieces of wax.

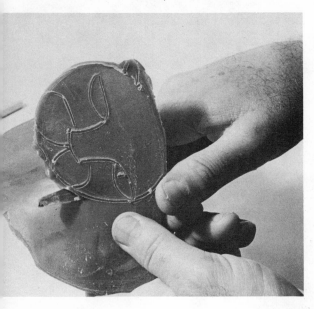

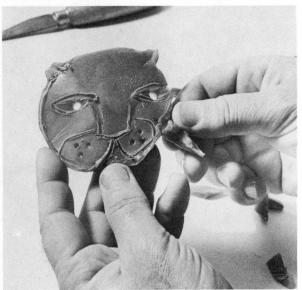

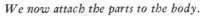

The head is curved around the rolling pin to give it a three dimensional quality.

Four pieces, to be legs, are cut from the cast-off sheet of wax. What we now have are separate pieces, the head, the body (and tail) and the four legs.

Another long sheet of wax is cut and shaped around the rolling pin to become the body and tail.

We now attach the parts to the body.

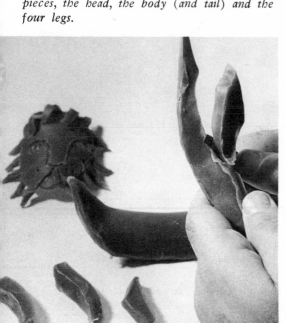

And so, in sheet wax, is our sassy, friendly lion.

Using the back of a pen holder (or you can still use your pencil point), we make some decorative spots—it could be a leopard.

With very little change we make a lioness, a companion for our lion.

Here is our leopard-lioness—with, of course, claws added to protect herself.

A bronze "pussycat" made in sheet wax technique—and cast. Cire-perdue method.

And a base always helps a piece of sculpture.

CHILDREN'S GAMES

In the development of a personal style, a sense of recognition is perhaps the most sought after single quality in art. Artists whose work has this sense of recognition do not need a signature on their work, for the individuality and distinctiveness of their art is their signature.

There are, of course, many factors that contribute to make an artist's work recognizable as his personal style. The basic quality is an amalgam of technique and theme. Technique is something that takes years of experience and dedication to develop. And there are no short cuts in the discipline of work. Theme, however, is a purely personal matter and the artist's own background and taste guide this. One cannot think of sculpture of the old west without thinking of Remington, or animals and Barye. Even in the more abstract fields, e.g., Calder and mobiles are synonymous.

The development of a theme can be an interesting exploration into the many possibilities inherent in a particular theme and many fascinating things can happen, including even that most elusive of all qualities, the emergence of a personal style.

For the purpose of illustration, we will take the theme *Children's Games* and, using direct wax sculpture as our medium, try to present a fresh slant on a familiar subject.

[29]

To make a little girl we form little pipe stem legs coming from a skirt bottom.
Right: *And, of course we add pigtails—or pony tail—or any hair comb you like!*
Opposite: *With a piece of wire our little girl now has a skip rope.*

Off to school—wax on wire structured cycle.

"Johnny-Ride-Pony"—Bronze.

"The Skip Rope Friends"—Bronze.

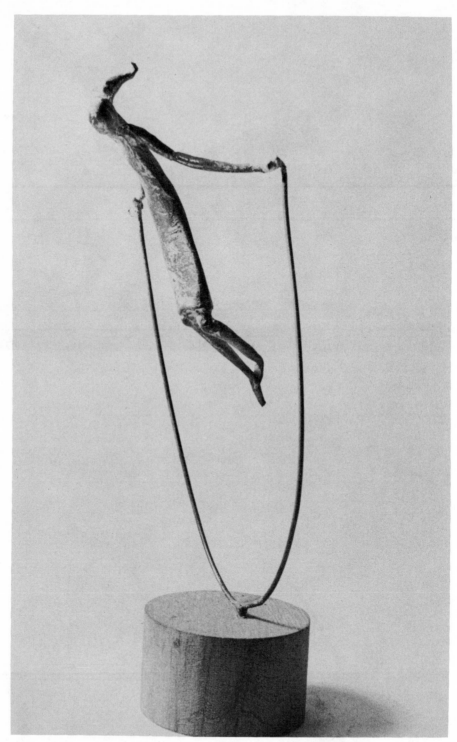

"Big Sister Skips Rope"—Bronze.

"The New Jump Rope"—Bronze.

"The New Tricycle, Sister's First Ride"—Bronze.

With the help of a wax seesaw our little boy and girl can play together.

"The Kite"—Bronze.

Little Boy

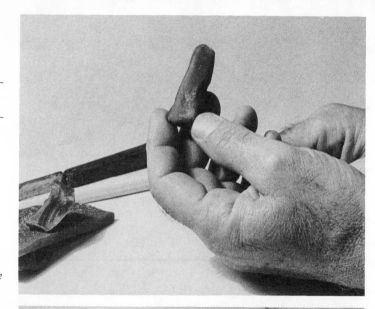

A small piece of wax will be our little boy's body.

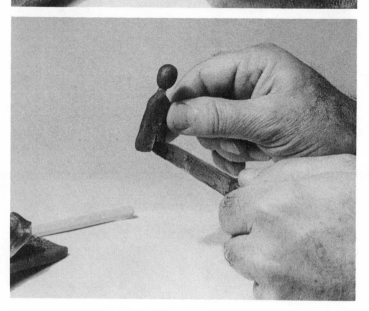

Pinch out a neck, and add an egg-shaped piece of wax for the head. Put it on the neck.

Cut into the bottom of the wax and separate the pieces for legs.

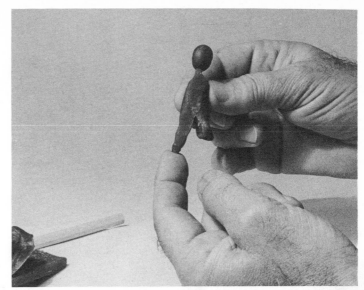

Taper each separated piece to form a leg shape.

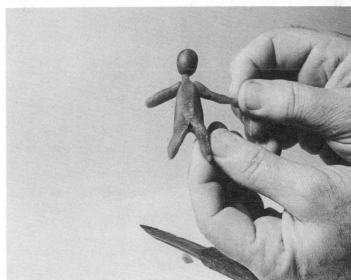

Two arms are added and formed to scale.

A pencil is used to form the V of the crotch which will separate the legs from the body. It is at this point that the legs bend.

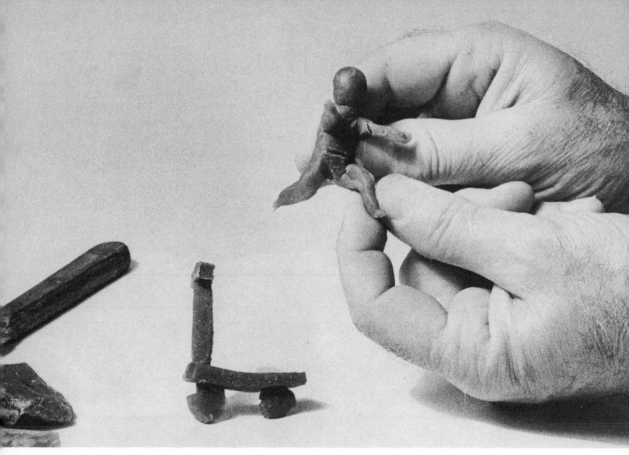

Make a simple scooter in wax. Then bend the wax boy until it assumes the proper action. Note that the leg bends at the V of the crotch.

Put the little boy on his scooter and attach them together.

This little three-inch bronze was done exactly as the wax we just finished.

THE FIGURE

Since the beginning of all art and its countless changes, innovations and styles, the one constant has been the human figure. And this is so despite the highly publicized avant-garde movements which rebel against all figure work, in fact, all literal works of art. The figure remains as the one single standard to measure all else. Man's goals and attainments change, but man himself is the same figure we see hunting for food in the cave drawings of prehistoric times.

The history of the world is recorded by artists who have portrayed man in his time and until man assumes a new form, the interpretation of the figure will continue to play an important part in the arts.

Wax has had its place in the recording of man's activities with the early castings from wax figurines, and it is fitting that we use wax to delineate the human form and articulate him to the movements that will give him life and meaning.

The wax figure illustrated here was literally created in minutes and done with no tool other than the fingers and a pencil used to give the impression of folds in the body. This particular technique of laying on pieces anatomically is especially well suited to wax. The small forms will not smudge or lose their crispness when the statue is twisted and bent to assume the various gestures and attitudes that the artist will try before finding the one pose that tells his story best.

Using a wooden base and a brass wire we can try to free our figure from the static weight of an inanimate substance and by giving him movement and meaning, breathe a feeling of life into the wax.

There is no face on this wax figure and there need be none. A face is not at all difficult to model but in art it is what is suggested that is important. And the mind and imagination of the viewer will fill out the face far better than your actual modeling could do. The same goes for the rest of the figure. The muscles are not true, the ribs are not correct, but all of these are suggestions to trigger your imagination. If the proportions are near correct, and the exaggeration not too abnormal, the mind fills in all the missing parts.

This particular handling of a figure is my personal approach, though after years of working this way I cannot remember how it evolved. But I do know that it didn't happen overnight. It is the culmination of years of trial and error, acceptance and rejection, and finally this particular style.

To those of you who are tempted to emulate these figures, I say fine. But use this technique only as a path to a style and technique of your own, which I assume you will come to with work, work, and more work.

The Figure

We will start with a wax stick figure and an egg for a head.

To identify our figure as a man we widen his chest and shoulders.

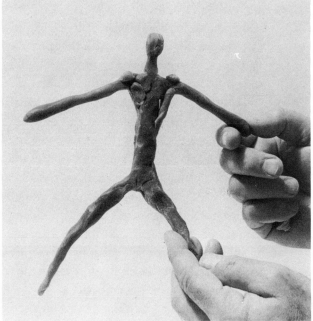

With small, appropriately shaped pieces of wax, we make a chest and add pieces to make a rib cage.

After having done the chest, ribs and shoulders, we add the stomach muscles and the hip or pelvic bones. It is at the hip bones that the body bends from the legs.

The leg muscles give a strength of character to our figure—a ball of wax becomes a knee cap!

The feet are made piece by piece—not only the toes but little balls to indicate the ankle bones.

Now let us stand our figure on a base with a piece of wire inserted in the base. The wire will be the staff to support the wax figure—now we can see him.

A pair of trunks, roughly sketched in, give an athletic look to our figure. A pencil or any tool can be used.

Now that we have made an athlete, let us bend him in movements that exemplify his sports—here he is a pole vaulter.

"The Tight Rope Walker"

"The Hand Stand"

"A Gesture of Achievement"

"The Flag"—a study in motion. The sweep of the wax flag accentuates the forward movement dramatically.

A piece of coral, an angry fish—add them to our athlete and he is now a merman. The trick is to compose all these units so they flow in a sculptured movement.

"The Bird Catcher"—a figure carried to a more studied finish, but done like the Athlete.

COMPOSITION WITH TWO FIGURES

What leaves are to a tree, so composition is to a work of art. It is the basic premise that makes or breaks the artist's concept. Composition is always present; it can be good composition or bad composition; it can be planned or accidental; and it can be called by other names. Design and arrangement are two words among many which add up to composition.

A simple analogy is composition in literature, and the key word is *compose*. For to compose really means to put together. A classroom composition is a series of sentences which, when put together, make a complete thought. In art, composition is a number of elements put together to make a recognizable (and hopefully, beautiful) piece of art. As a matter of fact, many artists refer to their efforts in art as "a personal statement."

In figure work a composition can be a single figure with all the elements; i.e., arms, legs, etc., arranged in the most graceful or flowing movement possible, or, conversely, in an awkward or stilted arrangement. For as I have previously said, when all the elements are arranged you have a composition, and good or bad, it depends upon the artist.

Two Figures

The possibilities of composition and movement with two figures are practically limitless. The important consideration in this type of composition is the balance.

The composing of two or more figures presents a fascinating challenge to a sculptor. I think that the single figure is the most difficult to compose, for what movement the human figure is capable of is prescribed. And the chapter on the human figure gives an indication of how best to approach the composition of the single figure. So to go one step further, we shall compose using two figures.

Any person who speaks in absolutes usually finds himself out on a limb, so anything I say on the matter of composition is open to exception. So, of course, is my personal approach to art. However, here are some of the basics that have held true for me for many years.

First, in sculptural composition, the more solid the mass the better.

Second, try to keep one dominant element.

Third, as we are dealing with three dimensions, keep the composition interesting from as many views as possible. By that I mean avoid making a one-view statue, if possible. (Sometimes it is not!)

I could write dozens of do's and don'ts which wouldn't mean a thing. So as long as direct wax is our means of communication I will illustrate the pitfalls and possible rewards with a series of compositions.

"Indian Hand Wrestling"

Siamese Dancer

Phoenix

Cat

The man on the bottom is called the "Understander"—an old theatrical term.

Here are the two wax figures. The problem is to compose them so that they relate to each other and in the relationship form an interesting sculptural pattern.

Here are two figures composed in an upward sweep of movement. The center pieces are braces, holding the wax in place prior to casting.

"The Acrobats"

The two figures composed in a "Pinwheel" pattern—it would be equally interesting if turned around clockwise.

STRUCTURED WAX SCULPTURE

Necessity is the mother of invention—and invention is the prime necessity of sculpture. Every artist develops his or her own personal techniques, and over a period of time these individual approaches coalesce into a distinct and personalized style.

This is to say that structured wax sculpture is nothing more than a technique born of necessity. In working direct wax, the problem of maintaining form without an interior armature called for a framework or armature that would not interfere with the sculptural composition. The use of cage-like frames to hold the wax led to experimentation in different shaped frames. In many cases the composition of wax looked more complete with the structured frame, and in fact an added dimension was achieved with no sculptural loss whatsoever.

Structure has long been used in sculpture as pure abstract form. The use of direct wax sculpture with these geometric shapes gives a meaning and direction to our sculpture as well as adding a new dimension to an existing sculptural approach.

Any writer's description of a process or technique in art must be inadequate, as art itself is a form of communication and a language in itself. It is therefore incumbent upon the artist to use his art to give substance and meaning to his words.

THE PROPHET

The head of a prophet is a simple, yet emotionally appealing subject for direct wax sculpture. Its simplicity of treatment brings it within the grasp of anyone not yet too sure of his facility with this medium.

We use a basic wire structure in the form of a Hebrew letter to act as a support for our wax prophet. We will model the head and construct the letter to act as an introduction to structure and direct wax.

The Hebrew letter ש is selected, not only because of its calligraphic beauty, but also by nature of its meaning. It is a symbol for the Lord, and it relates directly to the subject matter of the prophet.

A simple egg-shaped piece of wax, suggesting the head, is placed on the structure to determine if it is approximately the right size. Too large a head will dwarf the structure, and too small a head will be overpowered by it. Assuming the size looks right, we then start modeling the head in wax. We add our nose, indicate the mouth with two pieces of wax for the lips, and establish the character of the prophet with the basic forms of the brows, beard, and hair. All this is done simply and without detail.

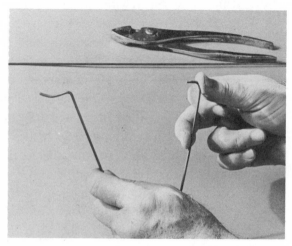

Wire bent to start the form of the Hebrew letter ש.

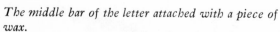
The middle bar of the letter attached with a piece of wax.

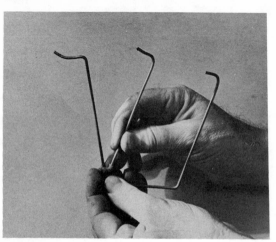

Set the letter up on a piece of wax so it can be seen as a standing sculptural form.

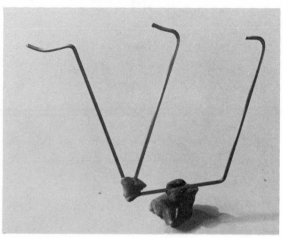

The head, when blocked out this way, is tried on the structured letter without the center bar, which would interfere with the head fitting in the structure. If it seems right in size and is generally correct, the center bar is added.

With soft wax the head is attached to the complete structure and the head and letter are worked into one composition—a process called "pulling together."

The final touches of the wax serifs and base make the wire structure assume the character and identity of the ש.

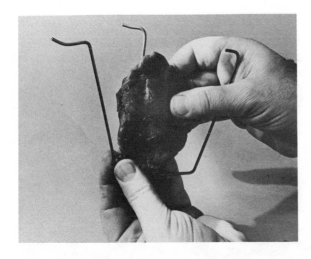

With a soft piece of wax we start the head, first placing it against the structure to make certain that it composes well in size and shape with the wire structure.

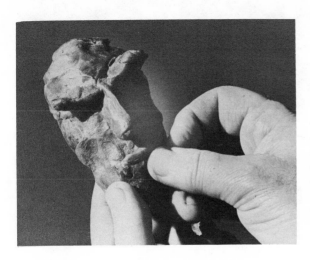

Now that the size of the head has been determined, we can block out our Prophet in wax. Roughly, without detail, the nose, eyebrows, and mouth are added.

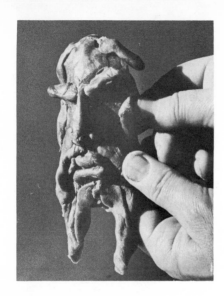

Keeping our forms simple, the hair, mustache, and beard are added to give character to our Prophet.

Eyes are added, then our rough sketchy wax of the Prophet is attached with wax to the two end pieces of the structure.

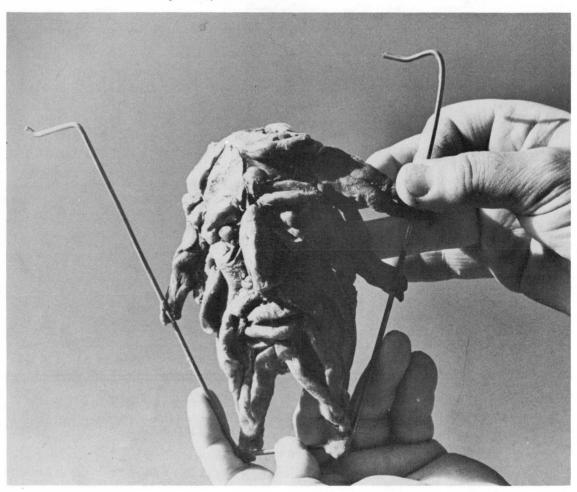

For the final blocking out process, the center bar is again added and the character of the Hebrew letter שׁ is captured with the addition of the serifs and the heavy base.

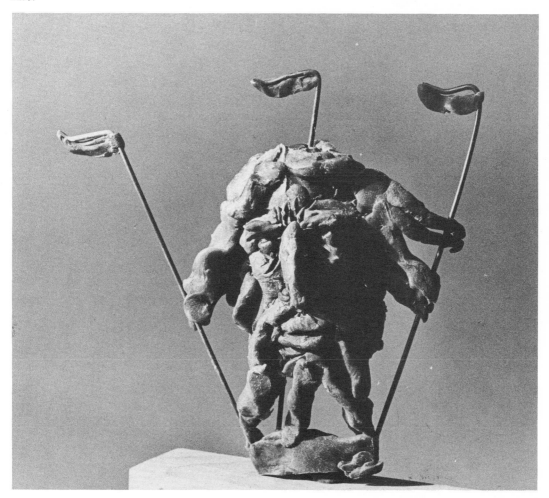

The refinement of detail and character give the artist's own personalized piece of sculpture.

A study of texture in wax—Head of a Prophet.

THE SWIMMER

The experience that most frees man from his environmental limitations of action is swimming. In water, the law of gravity is minimized and the freedom of movement and action brings us the closest to the feeling of suspension in space that the average person can reach.

Sculpture, by nature of its being a medium of mass, is as earth-bound by these laws of gravity as is man himself. The utilization of structure, with its airiness and open space-form, is one of the best suited devices to simulate this feeling of floating.

Using a heavy wood base, in this case a two-inch thick piece of soft pine, wide enough to hold the structure, we drill holes to hold the dowels that we shall use as our frame. Needless to say, anything that will act as supports can be used: welding rods, brass rods, umbrella ribs, wire, etc.

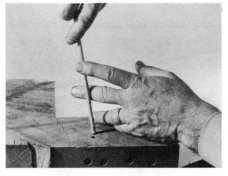

The Swimmer

Wooden dowels are inserted into holes, drilled at the desired angles, in a wooden base.

The height and composition of the structure are determined.

The dowels, or struts, can be easily attached to each other with rubber bands.

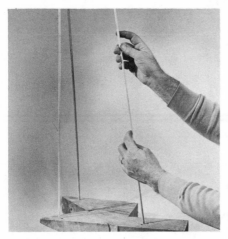

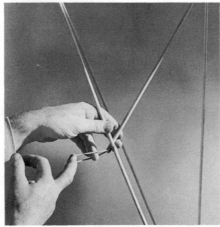

We shall use ¼″ wood dowel sticks to form our basic structure. To hold the dowels together at the meeting points, we can use rubber bands, although a piece of soft wax is a good temporary expedient to see how the structure will look. A more permanent binding can be used later.

Whatever shape or form the wax is to take, its size and compositional flow should correspond to the structure. In order to explore an exercise in weightlessness, we will make an undersea swimmer. The structure will free the wax from the necessity of using any form of base to support the figure. We must keep in mind, however, that the structure should have a shape of sufficient interest so that its use as a support is only incidental. A wax figure, on any conventional base has a more definite "front" view, but the use of structure gives interest from many more views because of the negative spaces resulting from the bisecting of the angles formed by the structure enclosing the figure.

A figure is modeled (as we have seen in a previous chapter) but keeping in mind that this figure should be composed in size and general shape with the newly made structure.

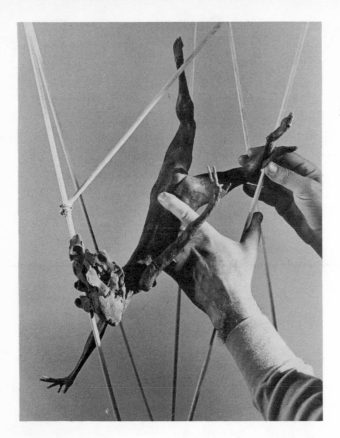

The wax figure is attached to the dowels with pieces of soft wax.

The wax figure is attached in many positions, and even twisted and rearranged until it fits in an interesting composition and looks sculptural from all views.

*Fish. Detail of "The Fifth Day," fountain
in the Hippodrome Building*

The Circus Troupe

The New Bicycle

"The Star Fish"—In this direct wax sculpture the Star Fish, holding on to the structure, helps blend the figure to the structure and to integrate the composition logically.

[71]

"The Undersea Chase"—This structure has freed the figures from a conventional base and allowed a complete flow of movement, plus an added third dimensional quality.

"Chase of the Sea Horse"—This direct wax sculpture was also done conventionally and is a small piece of sculpture. The structure has enlarged the area of vision and the feeling of the vastness of the sea.

HORSE AND RIDER

Composition in its true sculptural sense encompasses more than just conventional arrangements of figures or mass. The impact of the scientific explosion has had its effect on the arts, and the contemporary artist is as much concerned with such concepts as negative space, as with actual form in its tangible sense.

The development of mass can also mean the utilization of our space, captured in open forms to act as balances and weights. This spatial development of a statue is as necessary to its total concept as the medium used to set forth its statement.

Within this frame of reference, we will use a wax study of "Horse

Horse and Rider

The basic wax—without any structure.

and Rider" to demonstrate the use of spatial composition. Needless to say, if the work we start with is not well conceived, neither the addition of structure nor anything else will change an ugly duckling into a swan.

It is then most important that our wax study be well planned. With the following series of photos, we will try various spatial compositions using different structural arrangements, but always the same wax sculpture.

The obvious changes, such as size, its orientation (that is, which particular view becomes dominant), and the patterns of negative space formed by the ribs of the structure played against the outlines of the figure, are all minimal compared to the one dynamism that occurs with the angular, explosion-like thrusts of the soaring structure.

The spear of the Rider is utilized as the dominant member of the triangle which will enclose the Rider.

A second triangle is formed above the first triangle so as to also enclose the Horse.

The spaces between the wax and the ribs of the structure, the negative forms, are as interesting in some instances as the wax forms themselves.

The umbrella ribs are arranged and rearranged in a constant search for the structure most compatible with the wax horse and rider.

One of the ribs of the structure is brought forward in order to fully three-dimensionalize our entire composition.

"The Horse Tamers"—*The turbulent movement of the horse and figures is captured and held suspended in the* formalized *design of the structure.*

THE STRUCTURED EAGLE

Any work of art is the end result of choice and alternatives, for once the theme or basic form is selected, the game of elimination starts. What material is best suited for this problem? Shall we have a square base or a round one? Does the arm look better this way or that?—ad infinitum. Every artist has his own sense of design and taste to guide him through this jungle of indecision according to his own sense of artistic security.

I believe every artist has his own credo and approach to dealing with this highly personal area. For my part, I have found one real truth—sim-

Eagle

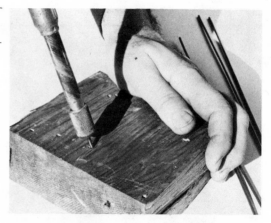

A heavy piece of wood is drilled at the angle desired for our rods.

The bronze rod should fit snugly into the base.

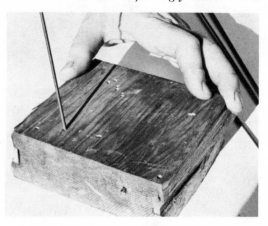

plify. Rarely does a piece of art lose by simplifying and getting nearer to the basic form. However, this is one man's opinion.

Let us take a definite theme and see if we can attack some of the possibilities inherent in this compositional problem. As long as we are discussing direct wax (that will be our medium) that's one decision made: and for our theme we will do an eagle.

Any approach to a subject that has been as extensively explored as the American eagle is beset with pitfalls, for to do this bird with any originality offering a fresh viewpoint and still keeping it an eagle presents a real challenge.

The following pictures are some of the steps and results achieved using structure:

The structure begins to take shape and assume an identity.

The thin sheets of wax being melted on to the bronze rods of the structure, using an alcohol lamp flame and a palette knife.

Detail of the body of the Eagle, made with thin sheets of wax in a tent-like shape.

The structure alone, as an abstract or geometric form. The same structure is used as the take-off point in an interpretation of the Eagle.

In this particular wax technique, the wax is melted in a double boiler, then poured onto an oiled marble slab, or piece of glass, in order to get large areas of wax about ⅛″ thick. Pieces are cut, and added to the structure to get the desired silhouette. This is called a sheet wax technique!

Three-quarter view. The structured Eagle done in sheet wax technique.

The silhouetted structured Eagle—completed in wax—sheet wax technique.

Left: *In this version of The Eagle, the spontaneity and sense of immediacy are in marked contrast to the highly disciplined linear design found in the structured Eagle.*

A sketch of a "Swooping Eagle" designed within a structure that is interesting in its own right.

A sketch of "Flying Eagles" suspended within a structure.

POOR'S EAGLE

A more architectural approach than the silhouetted wax pieced within a structure, is the more solid simplification.

In this type of work the structure is also an armature that prescribes the design, and the wax is used to give volume as well as dimension to the stated form.

Treatment of the form can be pure design. An example of this is the solution to the back of the eagle, which is a negative form. The space between the towering wings replaces what would have been a body, yet the concept carries out the illusion. Why take away from the strength of the statement by spelling it out, when you can trigger the imagination by implying the same thing?

I personally like to see the visible parts of a structure, even though they are not sculpturally necessary. I feel that the structural components are a part of the whole and in themselves are beautiful and honest parts of the eagle.

Many people would not agree with this—and their opinion is as valid as is mine—but that's what makes art interesting, and only time will be the judge.

The structured Eagle—conventionalized for architecture.

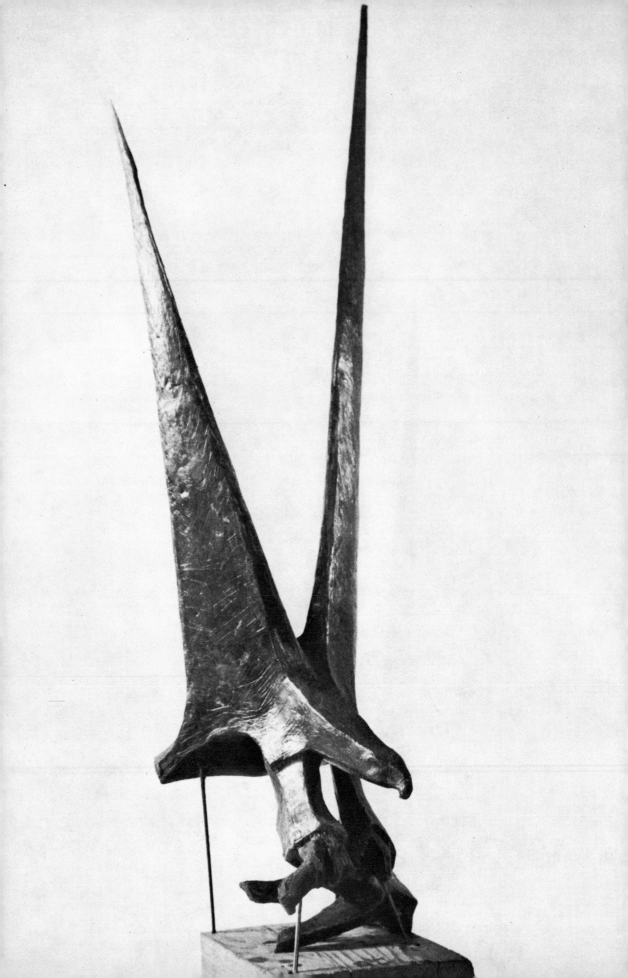

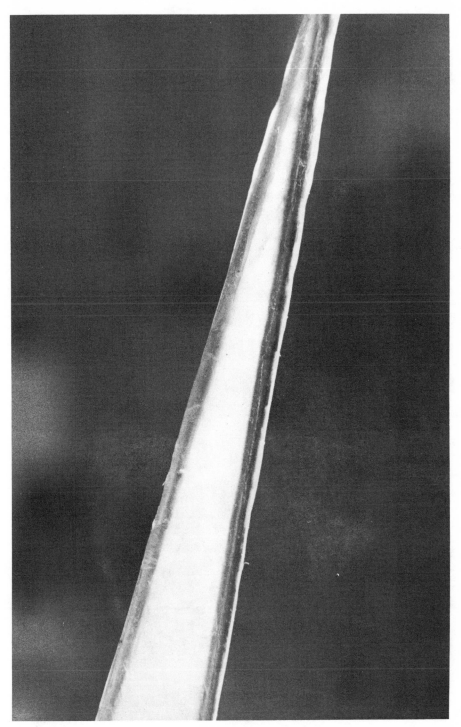

In this X-ray like photo a piece of the Eagle's wing is shown with the rods inside the wax.

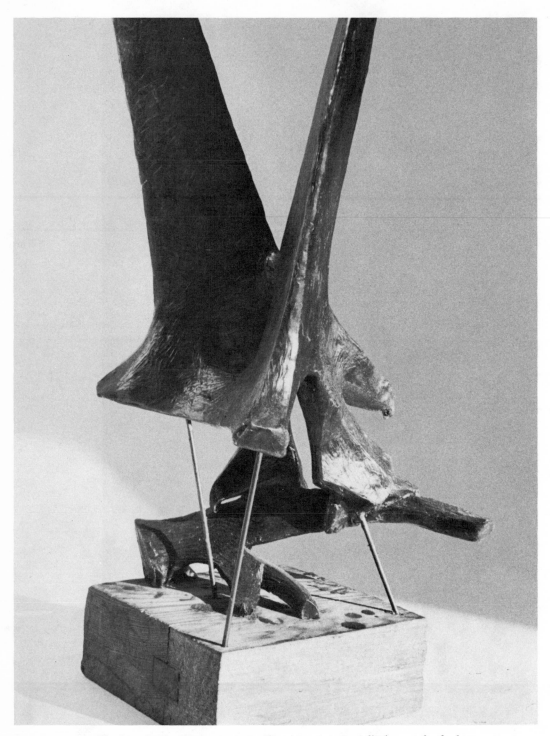

Back of Eagle. The conventionalization of forms eliminates the body.

The structure, which also constitutes the armature, gives an unorthodox but un-usual and honest appearance to this statue.

NATURAL STRUCTURE

The term "natural" is used in the sense of a normal necessity to the design. An example of this would be a statue of aerialists in which the use of the high wires from which the figures swing or suspend are essential to the statue itself. Although the wires are pure structure, they are also natural parts of the composition.

The following are a few examples of wax sculpture that lend themselves to structure surprisingly well.

In "Children's Games," the hoops and poles that are part of the play life of children become a decorative motif, and the children's accents within the pattern.

"Children's Games"—detail.

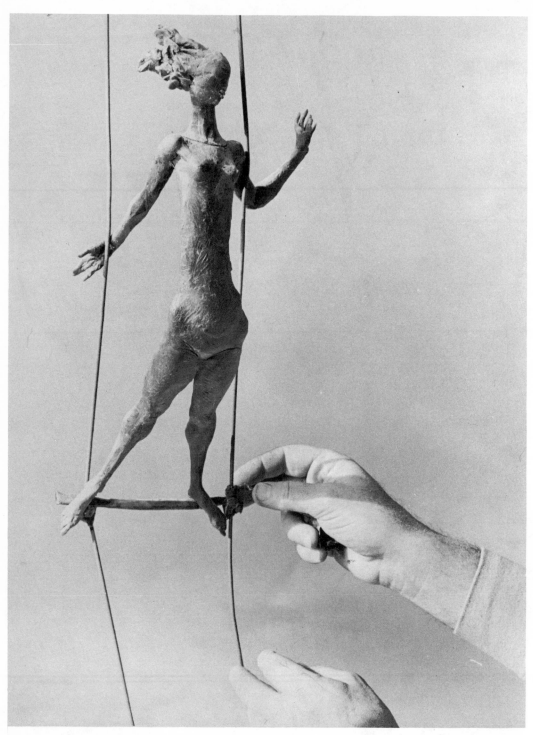

The wax statue of the Trapeze Aerialist being attached to a wire structure which will balance in space from a weighted base. Without this structure the wax is meaningless.

"The Aerialist"—structured suspension.

THE SKETCH MODEL

Any artist who works seriously will make dozens, even hundreds, of sketches before committing his idea to a large and final form.

In the two-dimensional field, these are often referred to as "thumb-nail" sketches. The sculptor will, of course, often do drawings as well as clay sketches in a preliminary period of exploration. In fact, the sketch drawings of sculptors are eagerly sought after for their spontaneity and economy of line. Rodin's drawings are a good example.

I have found, over the years, that wax, as in the thumb-nail sketch has many advantages that make it an almost perfect sketch medium.

Briefly, the wax will hold its shape regardless of the delicacy and com-plicacy of the composition.

The sketch model can be kept indefinitely, and with very little care. As a matter of fact, I have sketches that are over twenty years old and in perfect condition. While many artists enjoy the ease and convenience of drawings, the fact remains that every change of gesture and move-ment requires a new drawing. Wax, on the other hand, has the flexibility of an articulated mannikin and will retain its shape while permitting the sculptor to move it in any position or in a more abstract area, and to make any arrangement of forms.

Being a three dimensional object, the wax model can be viewed from all sides, or from any angle, and tested in all lights.

With a piece of soft, pliable wax the artist has, actually, a way of thinking with his fingers.

Speaking for myself, I cannot conceive of reaching a solution to a sculptural problem in a better way. These thumb-nail sketches are fast, easy enough to do, and strong enough to retain their shape, thus pro-viding the artist with a number of approaches to a given problem—all in three dimensional form, to be evaluated and measured against each other until a final, and hopefully, outstanding sketch is selected.

Here are a few ways I have used wax as a vehicle for "quick ideas," and then the later, more thorough study—in some cases, even the larger and more important commissions when necessary.

Sketch Model

The rough sketch in wax of the St. Christopher Statue—the final large statue is in wood.

Five preliminary wax sketches for the Holy Mother Chapel. There were actually fourteen sketches made—these were the first group. Right: Clay model of the Holy Mother for the Chapel, Father Judge Seminary—this design was selected from a group of over one dozen wax sketches.

Wax sketch for "Centaur and Dryad."

Plastiline model of "Centaur and Dryad" from the wax design.

Final wax sketch for the Mt. Sinai Temple.

"*The Torah is a Tree of Life*"—*Heroic bronze for Mt. Sinai Temple of Bergen County, Tenafly, N. J.*

Detail: This heroic bronze was first conceived as a small wax sketch.

THE ABSTRACT-
PURE FORM

The horizons of sculpture have extended, and in recent years the search for new means of expression has given new dimensions for the sculptor to work with. For many, the classic figure in its literal representation does not answer the problem of expression in today's terms.

Sculpture, always concerned with the occupation of space, has become the leading medium for the exponents of the abstract, nonobjective school of art. Breaking away from the normal use of the figure has, of course, led to the use of new media as well as the formulation of new concepts. The subject of the new concept in sculpture is so vast that no one treatise could adequately give it its just due. So I trust I will be forgiven for touching upon this area briefly.

Regardless of what school of art you belong to, or what you believe to be "The True Art," the one constant is still design. And while design is one of the important considerations in classic or conventional sculpture, it is the sole basis for the abstract sculptor. For in the occupation of space with pure form, only a design that sculpturally balances and reads from all views can be valid.

To those of you who are concerned with working in abstract shapes, wax should be especially welcome as a medium for thinking out shapes, forms and relationships. The use of sheet wax parallels very closely the technique used in welding sheet iron and steel. And so for this particular facet of nonobjective sculpture we will construct a few small sketch models in wax to show the affinity of wax to form, and perhaps open the way to an exciting new experience to the sculptor uninitiated to the experience of playing with pure form and space.

Abstract

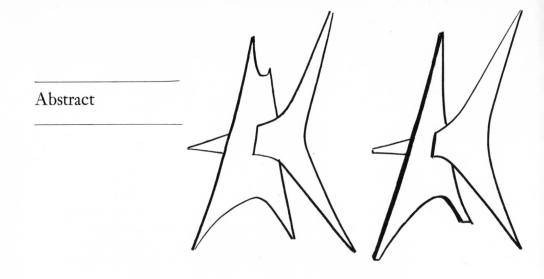

With a drawing as reference, the first form is drawn on a sheet of wax.

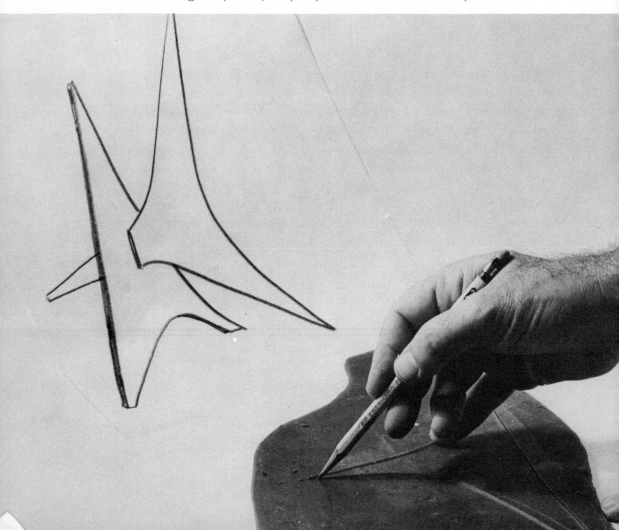

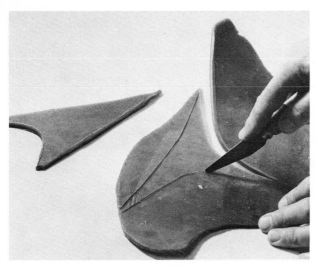

The second form is cut from another sheet of wax.

The two forms, firmly interlocked, become a single sculptural form capable of standing without support.

A notch is cut in the wax, as shown in the drawing, allowing the forms to mesh together firmly.

By tilting the notched form so that the legs are splayed away from the triangle form, we have a different composition.

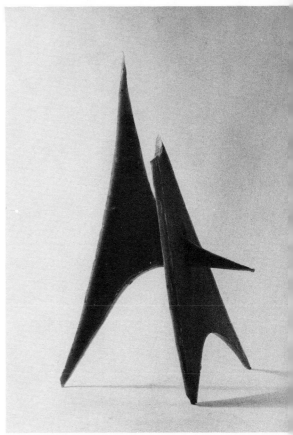

This final sketch seems the best, for while only ten inches high, it seems to have a monumental quality—and this is the true test of a sketch model.

The Minyan

The Wrestlers

Europa and the Bull

TEXTURE

One of the least appreciated and yet most important of all qualities in a wax or bronze is texture. For what chiaroscuro is to painting—that important element of light and dark—texture is to sculpture. Although the primary concern of a sculptor is mass and form, the surface treatment of all form is of paramount concern. The very nature of wax, its responsiveness to touch, and its ability to capture even the most subtle of textures, gives the artist ample opportunity to breathe life into his work with surfaces that can make his work vibrate.

Modeling, in the true sense of the word, is adding on piece by piece until the desired form is reached. Sculpture is carving away, as from a large stone or piece of wood, until the desired statue is attained. We also use the word sculpture to embrace all forms of the art.

With wax we are, of course, modeling, and the very fact of adding piece by piece in itself gives a texture that is somehow life-giving in its feeling of spontaneity. Many artists let the wax give its own texture and use practically no tools. In other cases, the use of tools or any objects to produce interesting textures can dramatize your work.

In working large waxes, I have used a soldering iron to burn interesting patterns in the wax, a blow torch to get a dripping wax effect, and I have even used sea shells by pushing them into the soft wax to get some unusual texture effects.

The use of open work—that is, building a sheet of wax piece by piece, and allowing some holes to appear by not completely closing the area—can give a freshness and a sense of immediacy to a statue. A bold and definite texture will do one thing; it will prevent a statue from having a smooth, slick, and over-worked look. Many artists, I among them, feel that very often smoothing, and the working and reworking of a statue will sacrifice freshness and freedom of style for technique.

In the words of a good friend of mine (a sculptor who shall remain nameless), "Are you doing art or taxidermy!"

PATINING WAX

I can only think of one reason to patine wax, and that is if one wishes to show what a bronze will look like when finished in a patine other than the standard wax color (which does look like a standard brown patine), or of course, if the wax is of a different color, or is discolored by candle carbon.

In any event, be warned of one important thing. A patine on the wax will prevent a good burn-out of the wax if you plan to cast it at a later date. Any impurities in the wax constitute a hazard for later casting, and the residue of a patine is usually a sludge in the mold.

First, and most important, do not start with anything that has a turpentine base, for turps cuts wax. For instance, oil paints are turpentine oriented and will not dry on the untreated wax. So the first coat on the wax should be a clear shellac, thinned with alcohol, and a bronze powder added to this thinned shellac. A statuary brown bronze color is the best. The other bronze powders are apt to get very garish.

This can also be bought in spray cans—expensive but very satisfactory for a good even coat of color. This will give an even but uninteresting bronze patine, so that a "touch" is needed to give an interesting finish.

In order to do the next step the shellac and bronze color coat must be thoroughly dry, for we are now going to use oil colors thinned with turpentine. If the turps get to the wax in any way, the wax will become soft and sticky.

For an antique green I put some turpentine into a cup and add zinc white oil color. This must be thinned out to an opaque white solution. Then squeeze a touch of yellow oil paint (very, very little!) and into this pale yellow we now add a soupçon, just the tip of a knife dipped into the oil, of a good blue (Prussian blue is strong, but good). Mix this until the color is that very light green seen on old bronzes, or those old roofs that have copper flashings and ornament.

This mixture you now have will be very thin and a very light blue-green. Brush it over the bronze colored wax. It will be greener in the low spots, and because of its thin mixture will run off the high spots giving a genuine bronze patine.

Now that you have the basic process, go ahead and do your own variations, for every artist jealously guards his own secrets of patining.

THE LARGER WAX-
THE CORE

The sculptor who likes to work in large forms using direct wax must consider the ultimate bronze casting of his work. The ideal wax model for casting is one with an even thickness, say ¼″ throughout the statue. In the foundry this is made possible in the standard lost wax casting by making a gelatine mold of the sculptor's model (which is usually in plaster). Into this mold of gelatine hot wax is brushed in and built up to the desired thickness—usually a maximum of about ¼″. Inside this hollow wax is where the core (the same type of investment used on the outside of the wax) is poured, so that the wax shell is literally sandwiched between two fire-resistant bodies. Later, when the wax is burned out, all that remains is the thin, even spaces for the bronze to flow into.

The sculptor who is working in direct wax is not going to have a mold made of his wax in order to make another wax, so he must make his own core and work his wax around it, and this takes planning. But first look at the diagram of a standard wax casting with the core. It is obvious that one must make a core that closely approximates the final statue—just smaller—so that when the wax is applied over and around the core, there will be a fairly even thickness of it.

The material for the core is easily available. The dental investment, bought through any dental supply house, is easy to purchase. Either ask your dentist or look in the classified section of the phone book. The bronze foundries use commercial investment of a coarser quality. In the less sophisticated foundries old bricks, ground up and mixed with silica and dental plaster (or any plaster), are used.

My suggestion is to use equal parts of silica and plaster, and you have a good, workable investment for your core.

I have worked large sheets of wax over mesh, and then the foundry has cored the wax statue. But if you make your own core (and you can make it around a mesh frame), your wax will hold its form much more securely until you get it to the foundry.

FROM THE FINGERS
TO THE FOUNDRY

Wax, as lovely as it is, still is a fugitive medium. It is subject to extreme heat, can wilt in very warm weather, and can be twisted out of shape by any mishap. And so wax is the intermediate step on the way to the ultimate permanence of bronze, or even the more precious metals.

Early man discovered that the wild honey he ate yielded beeswax from the honeycomb and that this beeswax could be shaped into forms, some of useful objects, and some of gods to be worshiped.

Exactly how man discovered the *cire-perdue*, or lost wax, method is of course not known. But we do know that by this time man was using beeswax, clay and molten metal.

It was then only a short step for man to form an object in the beeswax from the honeycomb and then pack soft clay from the river banks around it. When the clay hardened, he put the wax object, encased in the clay, into a fire and watched the wax melt and run out of the clay, leaving a mold or negative of his original wax model. Then, by pouring molten metal into the hole in the clay that had been formed when the wax ran out, he achieved his first "lost wax bronze"!

Cire-perdue, which of course is the French word for lost wax, has become synonymous with Benvenuto Cellini, the great Renaissance sculptor and goldsmith. However, long before Cellini, and in different parts of the world, this process was already well established. In such places as Egypt, India, China, Peru, and Mexico, lost wax casting was well in use.

Some of the work was done in a primitive and simple method, and in the course of time other cultures developed a more sophisticated approach to this process. However, the basic problems have been the same in all ages.

The model must be embedded in the investment, that is, the material around the wax, and yet have sufficient opening for the wax to run out, and later for the metal to be poured in. The basic problem is that with one opening air is often trapped and the flow of the bronze into the mold is impeded.

In this basic method, a rod of wax is melted onto an inconspicuous part of the model and this rod is extended so that it will reach to the outside surface of the investment after it has been placed around the wax. The end that comes out of the investment is shaped like a cone, so that when the wax is later melted, this rod becomes the channel into which the bronze will flow, and the cone is the mouth into which the bronze can easily be poured.

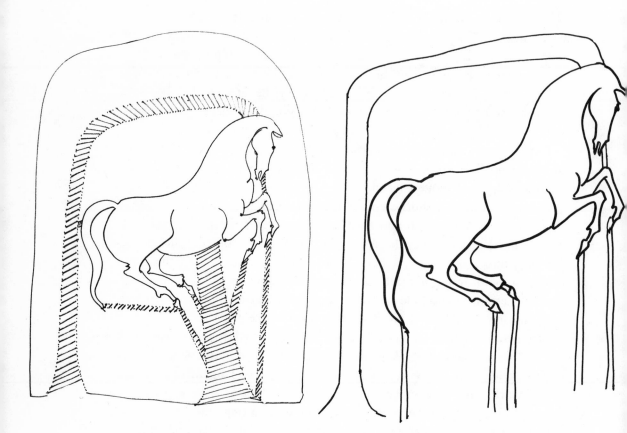

The accompanying sketch will more easily explain this.

Today, with our technological advances, lost wax casting has changed somewhat. There are many new methods, as well as innumerable advances in the original techniques. I will try to take you through one of the newer methods—centrifugal casting in lost wax, and then one of the older gravity-flow methods which is still used today.

In the back of this book are listed a number of foundries that cast from wax. Some are centrifugal, some use ceramic shell method, and others use a classic gravity flow. Take your pick.

UNTIL THE FOUNDRY

A problem that comes up too often for comfort is how to keep the wax statue from wilting out of shape and held together until it goes to the foundry. Some artists use a refrigerator and, in fact, one of the better bronze foundries in the New York area, where it gets pretty hot in the summer, has a large commercial-type refrigerator where the waxes are stored until casting. Another good foundry has an air conditioned wax room and a deep root cellar where waxes are stored. But what does the poor sculptor do with his wax masterpiece in the hot dog days until casting?

As I said, there is the refrigerator, but this has its drawbacks, for which needs the space more, the butter or the wax? The best method is to use bracing. This will hold the average wax statue pretty firmly.

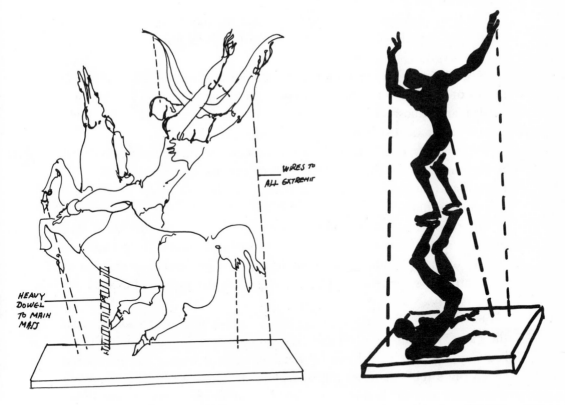

WIRES TO
ALL EXTREMIT

HEAVY
DOWEL
TO MAIN
MASS

However, the best method I have found I first saw in a foundry in Florence, Italy, where the summers get brutally hot. The waxes are kept in a large bathtub filled with water, where the buoyancy of the wax keeps the model suspended in the water—a foolproof method. Of course, not everyone, in fact, hardly anyone, has an extra bathtub that will not be needed for months at a time. So how about a laundry tub, or an inflatable child's swimming pool? There are dozens of ways to utilize this method.

I personally use a root cellar in my home, but in the studio I use the water suspension method and I think it is great.

CENTRIFUGAL CASTING

This method, comparatively recent in its use for sculpture, has been used industrially for quite a few years. The words centrifugal and precision casting are interchangeable terms. The exactness and delicacy that are needed in modern industrial work were made possible by the use of the "lost wax" method of the art world combined with the industrial use of the centrifuge.

The basic principle of this method is that the molten metal is shot into a mold by centrifugal force, as opposed to the metal going into the mold by gravity flow.

Dentists needing a precision tool for the faithful reproduction of a wax model of teeth, found the centrifugal casting process exactly what was needed, and almost all gold and silver dental work is done by dental technicians or the dentist himself by this simple process.

There is only one drawback in this process for the sculptor. And that is the limitation of the size bronze than can be cast centrifugally. No more than four or five pounds of bronze can be cast safely in a flask—that is, one mold.

The reason for this is evident when one sees how the bronze is shot into the mold from the crucibles by centrifugal force. More than five pounds of metal would break right through the investment as the arm of the centrifuge spins around. The accompanying diagrams will explain this more clearly.

One question that arises, of course, is how a person can know what the statue, with all the gates and excess bronze sprues, will weight. There is a way; the wax model can be weighed and the bronze can be figured at ten times the weight of the wax. Therefore, no wax model weighing more than one-half pound can safely be cast in the standard centrifuge. There are many casters experimenting with larger flasks, and some successfully, but the standard limitation as of this writing is five pounds of bronze.

While five pounds of bronze seems to indicate a very small statue, the fineness and delicacy of the cast refutes this. A mass of seaweed composed of many thin components will weigh very little though measure quite tall.

The flasks, which govern the size of the castings, are of different shapes. But they range from the small flask the size of a soup can, to the tin can that holds a gallon of shellac. But figure on a maximum of eight inches in height.

There is nothing to stop you from making a larger model cut into pieces that will fit into the flasks. Then after casting, silver solder all pieces together. For, after all, that is what is done on all large standard bronze castings.

The reason for the term "lost" wax is that the wax is melted out of the mold and therefore "lost". There is another reason rarely mentioned but still to be considered, and that is the possibility that for any one of a hundred reasons, the bronze will not be good. It can break through the investment, be too pitted, or perhaps not flow—and so dear friends, "Lost Wax."

Centrifugal Casting

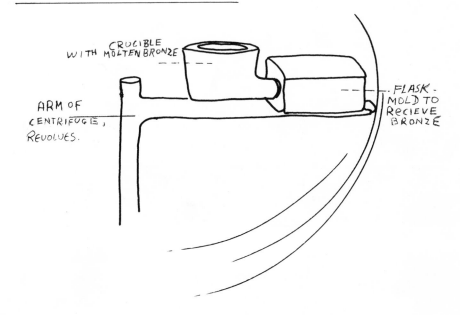

CRUCIBLE
WITH MOLTEN BRONZE

ARM OF
CENTRIFUGE,
REVOLVES.

FLASK -
MOLD TO
RECIEVE
BRONZE

The flasks, filled with investment, being covered by the vacuum machine, which vibrates the flasks and then by suction eliminates all bubbles from the investment.

"The Artist and the Caster"—The author and Dan Hudak, head of General Casting, discussing the best way to gate a delicate wax.

Still room for one more wax! So we add a little girl. All this will be far less than five pounds of bronze when cast. Now we close the flask.

A wax horse being gated for a centrifugal casting. The main gate will be in the heaviest part (the body). An electric heating tool is used to fuse the wax.

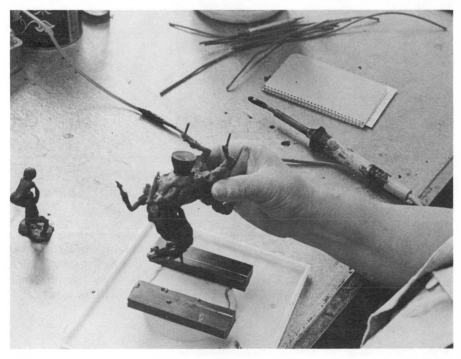

Runners, or small gates, are added to insure the bronze running into all parts of the mold after the wax has been burned out.

Pouring investment into the flasks which hold the wax models, completely gated and on the wax button.

We lower the flask on the base with the waxes to make sure the wax clears all sides of the flask by at least one-half inch. This insures enough investment around the wax.

Hot wax being poured into base, around button and gates holding the waxes. This insures the flask being air tight when put together.

The centrifugal flask has room for more than just the horse. We fit another wax on the base or main gate. Notice the runners from the horse's hoofs to the main gate.

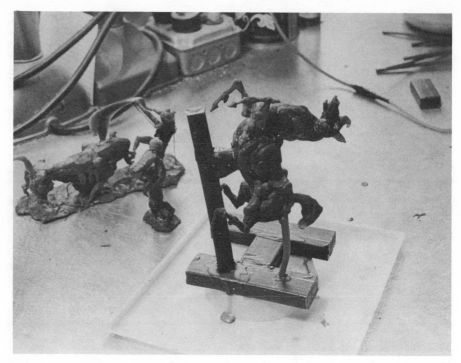

The plastic lid of the flask with the button in the center from which we gate the horse. The button receives the mouth of the bronze crucible in the casting.

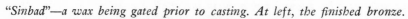

"Sinbad"—a wax being gated prior to casting. At left, the finished bronze.

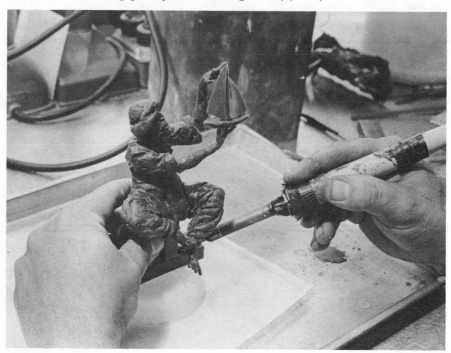

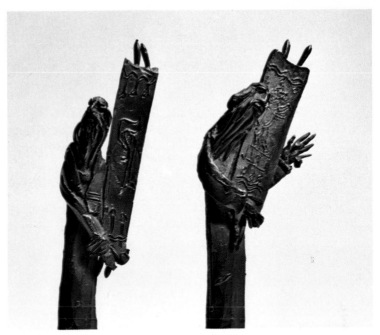

The Two Torahs

The Bullfight

The Prophet

Rearing Horse

Sinbad

CERAMIC SHELL CASTING

One of the newer and more sophisticated of the casting processes is the ceramic shell. The basic principle of this method is, briefly, as follows:

A wax model, to be cast in bronze (or any other metal), is dipped into a solution composed of a binding liquid, fine sand, and silica. This is allowed to dry and then is redipped. This process is repeated until a thin shell is formed around the model. When the wax is burned out of the model, the shell-like investment reacts like a ceramic and hardens to a strength great enough to contain the molten metal that will be poured into it to replace the wax.

In an actual casting I observed, the wax was first dipped into a binding solution then into a fine sand which adhered to the binder, then the silica, and all this built into a thin (quarter-inch or less), stucco-like covering. The only problem I saw was getting the bronze out of the ceramic shell, for unlike the ordinary investments used in ordinary bronze casting, the ceramic shell was very hard and did not easily dislodge but stayed in the undercuts. However, that may have been an isolated problem in the piece I saw being cast.

The advantages of this process are very evident: the ease of investing the model, the lightness in weight plus the strength of the mold, and with all this a cast that has all the perfection of detail found in the more familiar methods of bronze casting.

THE "DO IT YOURSELF" HOME FOUNDRY CASTING

The entire subject of bronze or metal casting is usually so complicated that halfway through an explanation of the process the average person says, "Forget it". It takes more time, patience, and energy, to say nothing of the cost, to cast a statue than he ever dreamed—and this is true. The art foundry investing dozens of waxes at a time, pouring a large number of statues at a time, and geared to do just this work, can afford to do a bronze for less than the sculptor himself (assuming that the sculptor has all the equipment). But seeing a fugitive medium like wax changed into a permanent medium like metal always fascinates the sculptor. And so, for those who wish to try a "do it yourself" casting at home from a wax,

A ceramic shell around a wax. The stucco-like shell is less than ¼ inch thick. The shell is an even thickness around the wax.

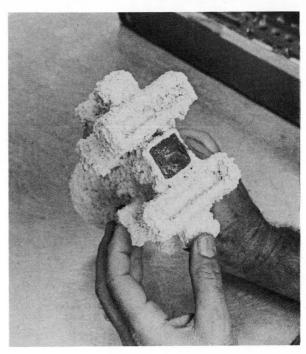

A group of industrial castings—ceramic shell over wax. Lower left hand is the bronze with shell removed.

here is a miniature casting process for SIMPLE and small wax castings.

We will use lead as our metal. Lead is easily procured, easy to melt (621° F.) and needs no sophisticated investments, only plaster. In other words, we will make a lead cast from a wax model. For this simple process, which I have done very successfully with the most basic equipment, I will use drawings to illustrate the few steps that it takes. But first let us make a wax model.

I would suggest a small head the size of a lemon. This will be sufficient to teach with. Now here is the equipment you will need and the drawings will show you how to use the material and equipment.

EQUIPMENT AND MATERIAL

1. The wax head—2″ to 3″ high.
2. Plaster of Paris—5 pounds.
3. Empty steel tomato can (or any can).
4. Asbestos gloves (or heavy leather).
5. Metal crucible pot to melt the lead in.
6. Oven, furnace, Bernz-o-Matic, Coleman burner, or any method to melt the lead. (I've even used a kiln.)
7. Tongs to handle crucible and hot tomato can—pliers will do.
8. Wax to make gates and sprues.
9. Hammer to break mold after firing.
   And that's all.

HOME CASTING BY STEPS

Here are the simplified steps in sequence:
1. We select our wax model, in this case a small head the size of a lemon.
2. We roll out our wax gates, first the large cone-shaped gate, called the sprue. The cone-shaped funnel facilitates the pouring of the lead into the mold later. We attach this to an inconspicuous place on the bottom of the head.
Then the two wax risers, as they are called, are attached to the other end of the head. These will permit the air to escape when we pour the lead.
3. Nails are put into the wax so as to hold the wax away from the bottom and sides of the can which will act as our flask.
4. The head with gate and risers put into a steel tomato (or similar) can with the ends of the risers and the cone-shaped gate above the top of

the can. The nails will keep all the wax parts from touching the bottom and sides of the can.

5. We mix plaster of Paris and fill the can until nothing but the risers and gate are visible.

6. After the plaster has hardened, we put the can in a pot or pie tin, wax opening down, into an oven—arranged so that when the wax melts it will run into the pie tin or pot—otherwise, a messy time!

7. After all wax has burned out of the mold keep the plaster in the oven so that it does not cool off.

8. Melt lead in a crucible, iron pot, or large iron ladle.

9. Pour lead slowly into the funnel of the warm mold until the lead comes out of the side risers, assuring you that it has not clogged in the process.

10. Let the lead cool then knock out of can, using a hammer or mallet to break up the plaster. Be careful not to hit the lead.

11. Cut the risers and gate, which are now lead, away from the head.

12. Clean all plaster from the undercuts, etc., and then, if all has gone well, mount your masterpiece on a nice cube of mahogany or whatever wood you like best.

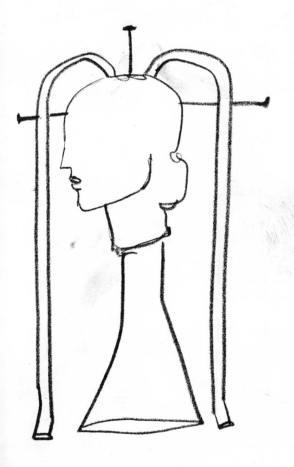 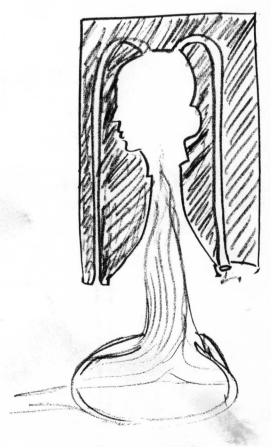

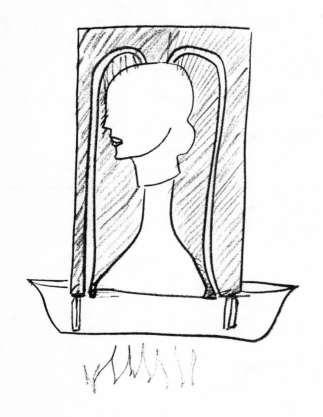

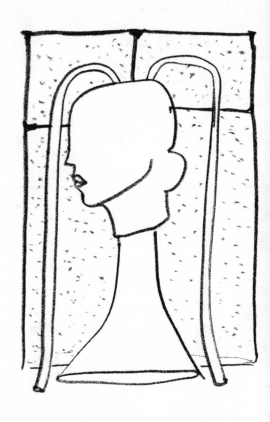

THE WAX MODEL FOR BAS-RELIEF
OR COIN MEDAL

Bas-relief, especially coin relief, is a very highly specialized and sophisticated art form. A sense of drawing, perspective, and delicacy is more necessary here than in other art fields. Because of the great importance of detail and texture, wax is very often used. It must be admitted that the average medallist will work in plasticine, cast, and then work on the mold—in the reverse.

However, many of the European sculptors (and some of the American sculptors) prefer wax. Of course, the great medallists, Pisani, Cellini, and the Renaissance artists, all used wax.

Miniature sculpture, Italian 16th Century. The Metropolitan Museum of Art, Harris Brisbane Dick Fund, 1936.

CANDLES AND JEWELRY

THE CANDLE

The words *candle* and *wax* are among the most synonymous in the English language. It is probable that the first ventures into lighting made by man were with the use of wax. Then later it was only natural for the candle to be used decoratively as well as functionally. And even in this day there are a large number of artisans in wax candles.

In this country we have a dedicated following in this particular craft, many of them members of the International Guild of Candle Artisans.

While the average person thinks of candles as made of ordinary paraffin, a petroleum derivative, the better candles are of beeswax. Good looking, well designed candles are as much in vogue today as they ever were.

There is one concern I know of that has handed down the art of fine candle making from father to son for generations and does a thriving business. The interest in beautiful candles will remain as long as people love beauty and graciousness.

The average candle is not an individually made piece, but in order to create an interesting model, the first piece must be handmade—usually a direct wax modeled piece.

DIRECT WAX, AS USED FOR GOLD OR SILVER JEWELRY

Since earliest times, precious metals have been treasured as adornment. The earliest jewelry of the Coclé indians of the Azuero Peninsula, and the Mixtec Pre-Colombian culture are good examples of the use of wax as the original vehicle of design in the new world. Of course we know well the great goldsmiths of the Renaissance. Today, wax and the wax synthetics are used in very much the same way as in those early and even ancient times.

Here are a few examples of ornament in many eras. But all are made by the use of wax modeled by man.

A 12" Florentine design candle from Ajello Candles, N. Y.
—Each leaf of this candle is individually modeled. Most candles are cast from molds.

Two pins by the author.

These were cast in gold from wax.

THE DEGAS
HORSE STUDIES

The genius of Degas needs no introduction, yet it is interesting to note that the personal quality that stamps his work in pastel and oil is just as evident in his wax sculpture. In fact, some of his waxes are even more alive than the finished painting for which the wax sketches were studies.

Along with the famous "Ballet Dancer," which has become an accepted masterpiece of sculpture, here are some less familiar but amazingly fresh and spirited studies of horses done in wax and later cast into bronze.

Horse statuette by Degas, also bronze. The Metropolitan Museum of Art. Bequest of Mrs. H. O. Havemeyer, 1929. The H. O. Havemeyer Collection.

French Bronze, circa 1921, by Edgar Degas, entitled "Ballet Dancer." The Metropolitan Museum of Art. Bequest of Mrs. H. O. Havemeyer, 1929. The H. O. Havemeyer Collection.

[147]

Another Degas horse. The Metropolitan Museum of Art. Bequest of Mrs. H. O. Havemeyer, 1929. The H. O. Havemeyer Collection.

Degas' "Thoroughbred Horse Walking," a bronze. The Metropolitan Museum of Art. Bequest of Mrs. H. O. Havemeyer, 1929. The H. O. Havemeyer Collection.

Bronze statuette, "Horse Trotting," also by Degas. The Metropolitan Museum of Art. Bequest of Mrs. H. O. Havemeyer, 1929. The H. O. Havemeyer Collection.

EARLY WORKERS IN WAX

Historically speaking, examples of early wax sculpture go back to the beginning of man's artistic expression. This being a book more technically oriented rather than a history of art, it is necessary to skim over entire ages and eras of art in which much valid and beautiful work was done with wax.

The few examples shown here, however, show works either modeled directly in wax or worked over in the wax for bronze casting.

The culture of the time in which each of these pieces was done is expressed through the medium of the sculptured wax far better than words can tell.

Roman statuette, a cart with oxen, part of a set of 14 pieces, dates from 1st century B.C. to 3rd century A.D. The Metropolitan Museum of Art. Rogers Fund, 1909.

Gold ornamental pin from Colombia, possibly Sinu. Courtesy of The Museum of Primitive Art.

Bronze horse, from Greece, 7th century B.C. The Metropolitan Museum of Art. Rogers Fund, 1921.

"Bastet, the Cat Goddess," from Egypt, one of the later dynasties. 900–300 B.C. The Metropolitan Museum of Art.

Italian metalwork of the 16th century, gold, enamel and pearls, attributed to Benvenuto Cellini. The Metropolitan Museum of Art. Bequest of Benjamin Altman, 1913.

Nigerian bronze, "Horn Player," of the late 16th to early 18th century. Courtesy of The Museum of Primitive Art.

"*Leopard Head,*" *17th century Nigerian bronze. Courtesy of The Museum of Primitive Art.*

Double-headed jaguar pendant, Panamanian Tambaga.

Miniature portrait bust of Victor Amadeus III of Savoy, colored wax sculpture, Italian, late 18th century. The Metropolitan Museum of Art. Gift of Captain and Mrs. William G. Fitch, 1910.

Italian miniature sculpture, wax, "Lady with a Mirror." The Metropolitan Museum of Art. Gift of Captain and Mrs. William G. Fitch, 1910.

SOME WORKERS
IN WAX

Almost every sculptor has worked with wax at some time or other in his career. For some it was just "another medium", but for others it struck a responsive chord and became a means of expressing a three-dimensional concept in a new and fresh manner. The average sculptor does not use wax for, frankly, it is less convenient than clay or plasticine, and above all, impractical for large work.

In spite of these considerations, it is surprising how many sculptors have evolved a personal style using direct wax as their medium. The work presented here is a cross section of many styles and is predominantly the work of sculptors I know personally. There are countless numbers of other equally gifted sculptors whose work I am unable to show, but this cross section will afford a slight glimpse into the possibilities of direct wax.

Abe Satoru, for instance, is a highly gifted sculptor, working in New York, almost exclusively in welded steel and copper. He uses direct wax for small work to be cast in bronze, to keep his individual style intact.

On the other hand, Robert Cook, who lives in Rome, works almost exclusively in wax, even to the extent of heroic sized compositions. And so on down the line. However, lest I fall into the easy trap of trying to explain sculpture with words, I will present a number of these sculptors whose work in wax speaks very beautifully for them.

"Where?", wax sculpture 9 inches high, weighing 9¼ pounds. Foundry: Alf Peterson, Venice, California.

"The Last Supper," bronze, 9" x 20" x 12", 1961, by Stanley Bleifeld.

"The Deposition," 12½" sculpture, 1963, also by Stanley Bleifeld.

A bronze entitled "Aspara," by Richard Bonce.

"Girl Tying Apron," 15" bronze by Bruno Lucchei.

Bleifeld's 20" x 15" x 12" bronze, "The Assassination of Julius Caesar."

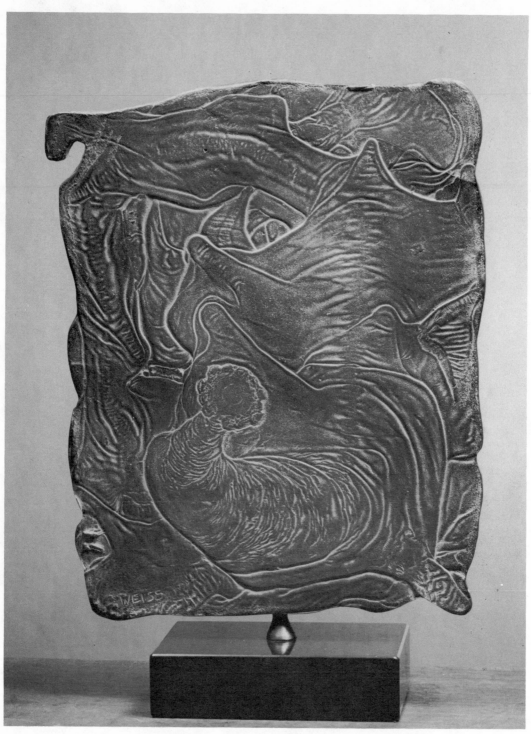

"Daedulus Labyrinth," by Sadie Weiss, is not, strictly speaking, a sculptured piece. It is a sheet of wax which was formed by pouring it, when melted, onto a sheet of glass that had been covered with a thin layer of water. Effects like this are possible when pouring hot wax on an even, wet surface. The beauty of accidental effects have a sense of immediacy that cannot be planned.

Abe Satoru's "Trees in the Shadow of the Shell," a bronze.

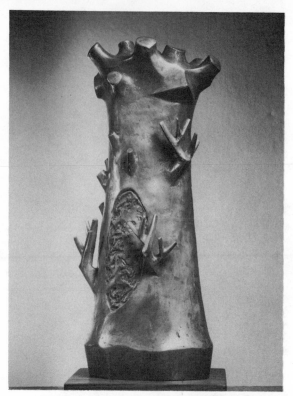

Another Abe Satoru bronze, "From the Old Tree."

Phillip Noteriani's "Rooted in the Absolute."

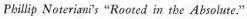

A bronze by Robert Cook, "Jacob #1."

"Wild Rocker," another bronze by Robert Cook.

Robert Cook's bronze, "Variation."

Another view of "Wild Rocker."

A 20″ bronze entitled "Resolution," by Robert Cook.

"Elysian Gate," a bronze by Sadie Weiss.

"Nereids," by Sadie Weiss.

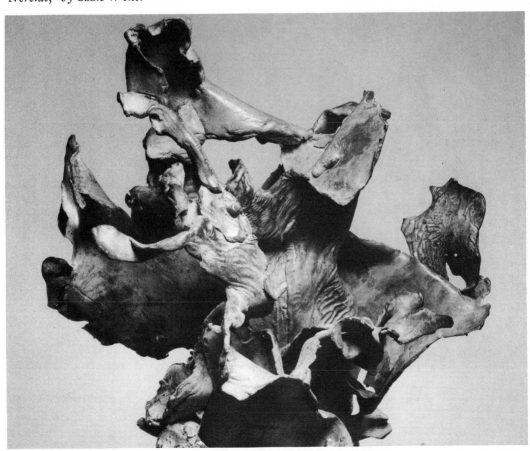

Hélène B. Proteau, "Chrysalide."

"Minerve," a 16" bronze by Hélène B. Proteau.
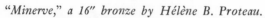

A bronze by Hélène B. Proteau entitled "Phébé."

SOME NOTES ON
THE PHOTOGRAPHS

The worker in wax will find that it will be to his advantage to be able to take acceptable photographs of his work for his own records and to be able to answer requests for illustrations. Wax sculpture is difficult to transport, even to a nearby photographic studio, and shipping a wax or a bronze can be downright hazardous. Many exhibitions and shows now request that a black and white print or a color slide be submitted with the application so that preliminary judging may be done without the necessity of sending original work.

The photographs I made for this book were taken with equipment and materials available to and used by the average amateur photographer. Ninety percent of the photographs were taken with a medium priced, single lens reflex 35mm. camera, using a tripod, one small portable 500 watt lamp, and a close-up attachment for "zooming-in." The black and whites were taken on fast panchromatic film (A. S. A. 400), and the color on slow film (A. S. A. 25).

Available light, daylight or artificial, was used for general illumination in both the black and whites and in the color, and the 500 watt lamp was used for modeling. The close-ups of the figures were treated as portraits and the modeling light was used to cast a shadow under the nose, illuminate the eye area and to emphasize the planes in the face. In the full figures, a camera angle was selected each time which would show the head and all the limbs to advantage. This took patience, for it is easy to lose an arm or leg or to fail to get a good angle of the head in the dynamic figure sculptures of Frank Eliscu. It was, therefore, necessary to keep making slight shifts in the angle of view, in the height of the camera and in the position of the main light until the best view was obtained. This meant moving the camera up or down a few inches at a time, turning the wax or the bronze ever so slightly, and then moving the light inches at a time for the correct modeling.

A very light background of "no-seam" paper was selected to give maximum separation between the wax or bronze and the background. (No-seam paper comes in a roll and may be obtained at the larger art stores.)

Any roll of paper will give the same effect of no line in the background. An incident light meter was used to determine the exposure, because a reflected light meter would tend to give a reading off the light background rather than the work. The indicated exposure was increased by one-half stop to offset the tendency of wax and bronze to "soak-up" the light. If the indicated exposure was $\frac{1}{30}$th of a second at f16, the actual exposure was made at $\frac{1}{30}$th at a stop between f16 and f11. A tripod was used at all times to make certain that there was no change in camera position after focusing and to permit a slow exposure with a "stopped down" lens to get the maximum depth of field when working with small objects. Maximum image size was used wherever possible. This is particularly important in color slides, where the size of the original image in the first exposure becomes the actual size of the finished slide. It is a good idea to retain the original slide in your files and have duplicates made for submitting slides to show.

Just one more word on the selection of the light background: I tried cold tone backgrounds and warm tone backgrounds and found that the warm tones were better than the cold tones, but then the light off-white background was best of all because it did not distract from the original wax or bronze.

DAVID ROSENFELD

[178]

APPENDIX

ART FOUNDRIES FOR LOST WAX CASTING

Renaissance Art Foundry	South Norwalk, Connecticut
Roman Bronze Works	Corona, Long Island, N.Y.
Modern Art Foundry	Long Island City, N.Y.
RAF Racine Art Foundry	Detroit, Michigan
Avnet Shaw	Plainview, Long Island, N.Y.
Fundicion, Artistica	Calzada la Naranja, Mexico
The Morris Singer Foundry, Ltd.	18 South Parade, London, SW3, England

GLOSSARY

Risers	Used in bronze casting. Made of wax, they melt away and permit air to escape mold.
Plaster of Paris	A calcined gypsum. When mixed with water it sets in minutes and is used in making molds and casts.
Ceramic Shell	A mold used in casting. A comparatively new method used for lost wax casting.
Flask	A metal casing into which the mold for centrifugal casting is poured.
Centrifugal Casting	A method of small wax casting in which the metal is shot into the mold by centrifugal force.
Gravity Flow	A method of bronze casting, it is the oldest and most basic form of bronze casting.
Patine	A coloring of any medium to simulate aging, or even to simulate another medium.
Lost Wax	A casting method in which the wax is melted out of a mold and therefore "lost."
Gelatine Mold	A soft, jelly-like substance used in casting. It is extensively used for intricate and delicate molds with undercuts.
Core	A solid form placed in a mold around which the metal is poured so as to produce a hollow cast.

Investment	A plaster silica preparation used as mold material in fine casting, i.e., dental investment.
Microcrystalline	A synthetic wax manufactured by the oil companies, as it is a petroleum product.
Sprue	A wax funnel used in lost wax casting. When melted it becomes the mouth for the bronze to enter the cast.
Unique Bronze	A bronze cast from a direct wax, using lost wax method, the wax having been melted away. The resulting bronze then is the only, i.e., unique cast.
Armature	A framework or brace to support the wax or clay when doing sculpture.

FRANK ELISCU

Frank Eliscu was born in New York City in 1912, and attended the Beaux Arts Institute of Design and Pratt Institute. He was later apprenticed to Rudolph Evans, has made numerous designs for Steuben Glass and executed a great many architectural commissions, both public and private. He is an Academician of the National Academy of Design. He is also president of the National Sculpture Society.

Mr. Eliscu has won many honors and awards. Among his recent commissions have been *St. Christopher* for the St. Christopher Chapel, New York City; *The Charger*, Dallas, Texas; *The God*, New York Bank, New York City; *The Torah*, Temple Sinai, Tenafly, New Jersey; *Abraham Lincoln*, Lincoln Bank, New York City; *The Naiad*, 100 Church Street, New York City; and *Man and the Atom*, Ventura, California. His *Shark Diver* is in the magnificent Brookgreen Gardens in South Carolina and he is also the creator of the famous Heisman Memorial Trophy, better known as the All-American Football Trophy. One of his latest triumphs is a three-figure sculpture of the astronauts at the Headley Museum, Lexington, Kentucky.

Mr. Eliscu and his wife, Mildred, live in a country house near Easton, Connecticut, which has a large studio for his work.